ISBN 978-1-330-45731-3
PIBN 10064963

This book is a reproduction of an important historical work. Forgotten Books uses
state-of-the-art technology to digitally reconstruct the work, preserving the original format
whilst repairing imperfections present in the aged copy. In rare cases, an imperfection in
the original, such as a blemish or missing page, may be replicated in our edition. We do,
however, repair the vast majority of imperfections successfully; any imperfections that
remain are intentionally left to preserve the state of such historical works.

1 MONTH OF
FREE
READING

at

www.ForgottenBooks.com

By purchasing this book you are eligible for one month membership to ForgottenBooks.com, giving you unlimited access to our entire collection of over 700,000 titles via our web site and mobile apps.

To claim your free month visit:

www.forgottenbooks.com/free64963

English
Français
Deutsche
Italiano
Español
Português

www.forgottenbooks.com

Mythology Photography **Fiction**
Fishing Christianity **Art** Cooking
Essays Buddhism Freemasonry
Medicine **Biology** Music **Ancient
Egypt** Evolution Carpentry Physics
Dance Geology **Mathematics** Fitness
Shakespeare **Folklore** Yoga Marketing
Confidence Immortality Biographies
Poetry **Psychology** Witchcraft
Electronics Chemistry History **Law**
Accounting **Philosophy** Anthropology
Alchemy Drama Quantum Mechanics
Atheism Sexual Health **Ancient History**
Entrepreneurship Languages Sport
Paleontology Needlework Islam
Metaphysics Investment Archaeology
Parenting Statistics Criminology
Motivational

FISH

IN

RIVERS AND STREAMS:

A TREATISE

ON THE

PRODUCTION AND MANAGEMENT OF FISH IN FRESH WATERS,

BY

ARTIFICIAL SPAWNING, BREEDING AND REARING:

SHOWING ALSO

THE CAUSE OF THE DEPLETION OF ALL RIVERS AND STREAMS.

By GOTTLIEB BOCCIUS.

LONDON:

JOHN VAN VOORST, PATERNOSTER ROW.

1848.

TO THE RIGHT HONOURABLE

LORD VISCOUNT MORPETH,

LORD HIGH COMMISSIONER OF HER MAJESTY'S WOODS AND FORESTS,

THE FOLLOWING

TREATISE

IS, BY PERMISSION,

HUMBLY DEDICATED:

IN ADMIRATION OF HIS ZEAL FOR THE NATIONAL WELFARE,
AND THE INTEREST HE HAS TAKEN IN PROMOTING

THE HEALTH OF TOWNS:

SOME IMPORTANT ARRANGEMENTS IN THE MEASURES OF WHICH WILL
MATERIALLY FORWARD THE OBJECTS OF THIS TREATISE

BY HIS OBEDIENT, HUMBLE SERVANT,

GOTTLIEB BOCCIUS.

INTRODUCTION.

In 1841 a short Treatise on Fish-ponds issued from the press, giving an account of many years' observations of the present writer : * it was intended to show the advantages which water-owners might easily derive from judicious treatment in improving the breed and breeding of fresh-water fish, and the large amount of good they might do to the community at large by the great quantity of wholesome food they might bring into the markets of both town and country.

There is no animal in the world like the fish in its power of multiplying its own species; but fresh waters require care and protection : they must be managed as well as protected, and they must be protected and managed on sound principles, or all rivers and streams

* 'A Treatise on the Management of Fresh-water Fish, with a view to making them a source of Profit to Landed Proprietors.' 8vo. Van Voorst.

running through populous countries will, in no long time, be wholly depopulated of their finny tribes ; and how and why I will endeavour to show, not theoretically, but practically, after long experience in the matter.

In again taking up my pen to give such information as I can on artificial spawning, breeding and rearing of fish, I trust that the number of years in which I have practised this art with perfect success will warrant me in attempting to show how rivers and streams may be restored to their former productiveness, upon simple, cheap, and unfailing principles, so that there never need be a scanty supply of freshwater fish as an article of food.

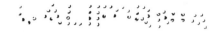

FISH IN RIVERS AND STREAMS.

CLOSE observation, year after year, has enabled me to ascertain the peculiar characters and habits of fish, and to become acquainted with the causes of their paucity in all rivers and streams; and the first and principal point to which I shall draw the attention of my readers is, the protection necessary to be afforded to them for a given period, which will, in return, well repay the fostering hand for this small expenditure of time and care.

One part of my system is to breed none but the superior classes and qualities of fish, the finest costing no more trouble to protect and feed than the inferior kinds. This is a subject of so much importance to the country at large, that I can only hope that the information and the hints I have to offer will produce proselytes, so that every river, stream and pond may be brought into a productive state of supply of this wholesome, nutritious, and cheap article of food. The main cause why all fresh-water streams become sterile in the end, if not carefully tended, is simple enough:

namely, all the smaller streams form the sewers of the ad-
jacent country, and fall into the larger rivers, and the latter
again act as the sewers of the towns and of the kingdom, and
are carriers of their congregated impurities finally to the sea.
The increasing population of human beings charges the
rivers every day with more and more foul matters, the refuse of towns and the agrarian districts passing into them;
and hence the destruction of the spawn, egg, or ova of fish,
but not of the fish when once brought into life. One cause
of this I shall explain chemically.   Water is composed of
one volume of oxygen gas and two volumes of hydrogen
gas. No life can be sustained without oxygen, let it be
animal or vegetable : consequently, when water becomes
thickened by other matters, a new compound is introduced,
which produces a new chemical action; and this is the cause
why all rivers and streams eventually become barren : for
the following is the result of such a condition of waters,
which it is an abuse of language any longer to call fresh.
The egg of a fish, in production, differs from that of other
animals, as the absorption of the spermatic fluids does not
take place till it has passed from the parent, and is then
left on its bed, hill, or weed, according to the description
of the fish, until the period of incubation has arrived; but
in the meantime, should the water become foul and change
its character, then the alluvial deposit in the water settles
down upon the pedicle or neck of the egg, hermetically

seals the same, and prevents the oxygen gas (the component part of water) from being absorbed and passing to the embryo, from which cause suffocation takes place, and the egg is, in the common phrase, addled. This may seem strange ; but the student of the laws of Nature well knows that oxygen gas is as absolutely necessary to life as it is the slow destroyer of all things. The destruction of the eggs of the trout from the cause just assigned I have proved to many friends, having shown them thousands in a putrefied state on their own natural hills or breeding-grounds; whilst, upon the principles I have to detail of my methods of producing fish, not a single egg is lost.

As I have not had the advantage of living for any length of time in the neighbourhood of a salmonry, I can only give my own views of the breeding and protection of that noble fish ; but I believe I shall not be far from the truth when I have shown what I have seen of the nature and bearing of the Salmonidæ. On the subject of trout and other fresh-water fish I can speak more confidently, as the practice of many years has given me such convincing results as are not easily refuted.

To do away with a deal of controversy as to fish being only fit for food in certain seasons, I will point out to those who may think it worth while to read these pages, that all fish differ more or less in their seasons : for instance, when fish are young, like other animals, they are more apt for

procreation than fish of older constitutions, and consequently begin to spawn earlier in the season than the heavy
or matured fish.   This will account, in some measure, for
the belief of many people that there are two spawning seasons for certain kinds of fish, which is not the fact.   Grilse
will run up to the head of their native river, preparatory
to spawning, in the month of August and September; but
salmon do not make their appearance till October or later,
so that the grilse's egg is brought forward almost as early as
the true salmon's spawn is delivered on the hill.   The full-
grown salmon egg is brought forth in March or April, earlier or later, according to the altered temperature of the
water at that time of the year.   This rule is applicable to
all fish bred in fresh water, and has been a riddle to our
best fishermen.   As soon as fish have shot their spawn they
become sickly, and are, as the consequence of their ill
health and weakness, infested with insects, both externally
and internally, and so continue for some time, till they recover their stamina, and shake them off or discharge them.
When again recovered and cleansed, Nature moves in its
usual course, and the fish is again called in season.

I have known young or maiden trout go to hill, or to the
spawning ground, in November, whilst matured fish of four
or five pounds weight would not spawn till the February
following, the former depositing some forty or fifty eggs,
and are thus actually in good season when the latter begin

to make their appearance upon the hill. The river which I have restored for many miles is the Colne ; but the most remarkable evidence of the results which I have obtained may be witnessed at Carshalton, on the Wandle stream, from which I have seen small trout taken by angling parties early in March, which were decidedly in perfect season, having recovered their condition, but did not weigh more than six ounces.

I will now draw the particular attention of my readers to the state of streams of which they are owners or fishers, if they wish to insure an abundant stock of healthy fish. As there are not many landed proprietors in our south country who possess more than five or six miles of river, I recommend, in the first place, that the levels of the falls be taken from the upward to the lower boundary ; so that a systematic husbandry of the springs, and a judicious discharge of the land waters by a back or tributary stream, may be obtained from the extreme point of boundary. This has a twofold benefit : in the first place, in keeping the thickened or land waters from the pure or spring waters, by which means their temperature does not become much disturbed ; for if the waters are blended, the fish become sick and cannot feed : in the second place, in making use of the artificial back-stream as a sluice, any accumulation of mud may be swept away with a very little management. I strongly recommend the removal of all trees and underwood from the banks of streams, to such a distance that the leaves cannot fall into its waters, as the decomposition of arboraceous matter produces humic acid gas, which is always prejudicial, and in some cases, when in excess, is destructive to all kinds of fish, as it interrupts their feeding and suppresses their growth. This will serve to account for the extraordinary fact, that, in private ponds exposed to these injurious influences, the fish have not increased in weight during many years. Wholesome water is of as much importance to fish as pure air to man ; and as impure air affects his health, so does impure water affect the finny tribe, and render them sickly and small. The depletion of our rivers is due, not so much to the disturbing traffic of steam-vessels, shipping, or any other river and river-side movements, as to the increase of our population, and the consequent increase of the refuse matters of towns and cities : for to this is to be ascribed the impure state of most of our fresh-water streams, as they are called by courtesy—a courtesy too complimentary. Strange to say, however, the very cause of destruction to the fish while in embryo produces them abundance of food when once brought into life. For instance, the very mud or alluvial deposit in our rivers and streams, which is an enemy to the embryo, breeds such myriads of worms, larvæ and insects, that when the young fish — all dangers overcome — find their way into it at last, they have no labour to procure food, and increase rapidly in size as a consequence of the easy life they lead: for it is a well-authenticated fact, that fish which have to toil hard in hunting for their food are bony and ill-conditioned, and never fat. Another strange characteristic of the finny tribe is, that on changing their locality they assume a colour suited to the waters to which they have migrated,—the result, probably, of the altered condition of light or electricity they have undergone in making this change: so that fish bred in a dark or deep water are dark, and those in a clear, bright, and shallow stream are light and brilliant, and hardly discernible therein.

A friend at Dorking asked me why it was that he could not breed trout, or indeed any fish, in one of his streams, although when he placed the fresh brood therein they grew rapidly; whilst in a second stream they bred, but did not thrive? My explanation was, that in the one stream the corruption to which the water was liable destroyed the egg, but afforded the brood abundance of food; whilst in the other, there being very little food, the fish had to work hard to obtain it, and were thus kept lean and small.

In proof of the extraordinary growth of fish when confined and regularly fed on food fit for them, I may refer to the two electric eels (*Gymnotus electricus*), now exhibiting at the Polytechnic Institution. These fish were imported six years back, and placed as objects of curiosity in the

Adelaide Gallery, in the Strand, and since have become
inmates of the above-named Institution. When brought
to this country they weighed about one pound each; but,
being confined in a very small space, and fresh *warm*
water daily given to them, agreeable to their natural element, and regularly fed, the largest of these specimens of
Gymnoti has grown to the great weight of between forty
and fifty pounds, the smaller one to about forty pounds;
and the cause assigned for this difference in weight is, that
the one fish was by nature the most powerful of the two,
and always claimed the lion's share of food thrown to them;
and it is a fact worth noticing, that the largest fish of the
two has the greatest power in giving the electric shock. I
have wandered somewhat from my subject in describing
these extraordinary creatures; but they have afforded me
the opportunity of showing what may be done by systematic
management in the feeding of fish, which is of more consequence than the inexperienced reader and breeder would
suppose.

I have seen trout taken from a stream systematically supplied with food, seventeen inches in length, which would
pull down above two and a half pounds; from an ill-stored
stream one of the same length drew no more than from one
pound and a quarter to one pound and a half: such are the
advantages of wholesome water and food regularly supplied.
Salmon of nine pounds weight will yield from 1000 to 1500

eggs : one of sixteen pounds from 4000 to 5000 eggs ! A trout of two pounds yields about 1000 eggs : one of twice the size double the number. The milter increases in the same proportion. A very beautiful provision is made by Nature to rid the fish of the film of the ovarium, to which the egg and the milt have been attached : an inflammatory action sets in, when the small worm called the Ascarides minor preys upon the part, and when the film is consumed they in turn become ejected, and then the fish recovers its wonted health and condition.

As regards streams for trout and coarse fishing, I must again remind my readers of the necessity of looking to the levels of the same, in order to form the necessary deeps, weirs, hides, submarine floats for artificial ripples, and all proper protections against the nefarious arts of poachers. Each ripple will form its own eddy, and as in each eddy the coarse fish congregate they become an easy prey to trout—as voracious a fish as any that inhabits fresh water. Some years back I saw a trout of twelve pounds weight, which had been taken near Teddington by a gentleman, and, on being embowelled for preservation as a curiosity, no less than seventeen small dace were found in his maw, which he had taken for his breakfast; and he finally was killed with a bleak as a bait. The dace were all whole, showing how recently he had been at his destructive work.

Where gentlemen desire to have a good and useful fishery, it is impolitic to allow the stream to become overstocked with heavy fish,—that is to say, where migration does not take place,—as large fish devour far more in proportion than the smaller ones, and constantly hunt and harass them, and hinder them from obtaining food. On this account, where many exist, the fishery is not upon a fair footing, and certainly not in a progressive or prosperous state. It were better that large fish, after a certain age, should be taken for food, or else removed for productive purposes elsewhere.

Many fishermen have doubted two things which I have advanced, but which I have been able positively to prove : namely, that certain kinds of fish, and especially the male, will devour the egg and the young fry as they come forth from the hill, and will fight hard to keep their prey to themselves. One of these interesting proofs was exhibited a few months since in the fishery which I have superintended for six years, and which is now the richest stream in the south of England. Even one of the fishermen belonging to the estate could not be brought to believe it, till on one occasion he was made an unwilling witness of the plundering habits of a trout which he captured, and which proved to be a male fish of about two pounds weight. In order to prove to demonstration the destructive effects of the deposits of a river when its waters become impure, I had a small bend made from the stream, which was well gravelled, and guarded at either end with perforated zinc plates, and the top covered over, so that neither water-fowl nor heron could ravage the hill. It was spawned with more than 10,000 eggs; but notwithstanding this seeming prosperity, not more than a dozen fry came forth, the remainder being all addled.

Fish which can obtain their food in an easy and peaceable way will increase far more rapidly than those which have to travel far for it. This I have explained to many gentlemen who have asked me the question — how it was that their trout were in condition not longer than two or three months in the year. The simple answer is, that during eight months of the twelve, they are, from scarcity of food, so starved that they are compelled to feed upon the smaller sort of their own fraternity, which, being swift of movement, become difficult to take; so that they are more like skeletons, or the heads and tails of trout, than fish worth taking, and do not get into condition till the fly-season comes round again. Nor are trout the only fish which practise spawn-robbery : for it is generally known to fishermen, that all sorts of fish are given to this piracy, and eagerly devour spawn and the young fry. At once to prove this, and bring the charge home to them, I need only mention that the roe of any fish in the spring season is a deadly bait, too tempting to be resisted, when offered to trout or any other fish.

At this very time of the year (end of March, 1848) the delicate smelt is being caught in the Thames, near Hammersmith, where this fish comes annually to spawn on the clean sands ; but who takes a smelt with an angle in the Thames in these days, as was formerly the case ? The smelt spawns between Hammersmith and Chiswick : the flounder also seeks the same spot for breeding, but, like the smelt, is becoming scarce, and from the same causes ; and this decrease is extending to every river in the kingdom.   It is high time, therefore, for the naturalist to resort to art to restore our fisheries, or they must eventually become extinct.

I will only touch, in passing, on the Thames, a noble stream, which might again be converted into a perfect salmonry, though the conflicting interests make it a subject of " non-preservation," and its conservancy a fable.   There are many other rivers as well, now running to waste too literally, which, at very little cost, might be charged full of stock, and annually supply a sure and certain abundance of fish.   I would not thus boldly venture these assertions had I not proved the subject by most decided success, by obtaining a better produce, and restoring a completely wasted stream ; and again and again shown the true cause of the depletion of rivers to originate and begin in the destruction of the egg, and not of the fish when once brought into being. Steam navigation, as I have said before, very little affects a fishery, as long as it is confined to the tideway of the river. Salmon never spawn within the range of the tide, if they have a free passage up to the heads or clear water: for it is there they desire to deposit their eggs in the shingle and clean coarse gravel. Most fish prefer to deposit their eggs in gravel or sand: but some, such as carp and tench, spawn among the weeds called Ranunculus aquaticus, or water crowfoot; and in this weed the egg becomes well entangled, and secured from the predatory appetites of other fish.

Salmon take one hundred days, trout fifty days, and many other fish forty-two days, to come forth from the egg, provided the water does not change its temperature during the period of breeding: so that it is not impossible to bring varieties of better sorts of fish from distant countries to stock our streams with, and I should say, from what I have myself experienced, with success. The temperature best adapted for spawning ranges from 53° to 56°, and at this warmth I have never found any alteration in the time I have stated, which may be relied upon as correct, and the true time in every case. Should this even temperature vary very much, then the egg, as the water loses its warmth, is sensibly retarded in its incubation. From this change of temperature I have known the egg of the trout to be delayed from fifty to

seventy days; and when the fry have at last made their
appearance, they have invariably been poor weaklings, and
puny in precise proportion to the time lost in their retarda-
tion in the egg. After a fish of any description has burst
its bounds into life, the vesicle or investing membrane,
which encompassed it in embryo, still adheres to the umbilical region, and contains a small proportion of the fluid
necessary to the sustenance of the then unprotected animal. This vesicle or sack is exhausted of its fluid in four-
teen days in trout, and in double that time with smolts, and
then drops off; and by this time Nature has taught these
little creatures to hunt for their food, and to avoid danger,
which they do by keeping close to the shallows. Carp and
tench spawn in June, at the time when wheat is in blossom,
which will pretty well indicate the temperature of the water
as well as the air. These fish spawn near the surface, and
this accounts in part for the difficulty of breeding them in
rivers and streams; though, when bred in ponds, and afterwards turned into rivers, they thrive fast and well, and are
better as food. And here, while I am on the subject of
carp, I may as well mention that the gold carp, a native of
the Eastern World, cannot breed or spawn under a temperature of from 70° to 80°, but at that they will breed luxu-
riantly: proper care, however, must be taken, or they will
devour every particle of spawn they have deposited. An
instance of this voracity I have from a gentleman who kept

some of these fish in a reservoir in his hothouse, but lost his brood regularly from this cause, till he placed some water-plants in the reservoir last year, and thus secured the stock. Few persons are aware of the cause of the death of these beautiful little fish when kept in the globular glasses, even where much care is bestowed upon them. It is simply this,—they become heavy in spawn, and not being able to rid themselves of the egg, for want of the assistance which plants afford in the act of parturition, inflammatory action takes place in the ovarium, mortification ensues, and death is the consequence.

Returning to the subject of the restoration of rivers, I should decidedly say, that all weirs should be wholly removed, or else that they should be formed upon such principles that every sort of fish may be able to surmount these obstacles, and ascend the stream for the purpose of spawning ; and this may easily be accomplished, if, in a navigable river, the one side be arranged for the lock, and the other side for the weir, of long inclination, without any further barrier ; or if again, on another principle, zigzag flights of steps be made, upon each of which steps the fish would have time to rest and recover its strength for a further leap, and, overcoming all obstacles, at last push forward for the clear spring or pure water. I point out these plans to show that, if artificial spawning, breeding and rearing be adopted at all, it would be wise, while you are about it, to give the

brood all the assistance you can possibly afford them to
perform their own final functions in the upper part of the
rivers, where, with these helps, the fry would be safely bred
up to their true perfection.   Salmon stop in the rivers
where they are bred (for this information I am indebted to
Mr. Olive of Gloucester) fifteen months before they migrate ; and they return in three or four months, weighing
pounds for months, and are then termed grilse.   These
facts have been very ably described by Mr. Young, who
superintends the fishery of His Grace the Duke of Suther-
land in Sutherlandshire.   At any rate, as grilse, they make
for their spawning-grounds early ; and, having few eggs to
deposit, they soon make for the sea again, and return to
their native stream as salmon, weighing from seven pounds
upwards.   They are now in their fourth summer ; and at
this age the ovarium varies in size according to the weight
of the fish, some containing ten thousand, and others
twenty thousand eggs !   I cannot forbear from asking,
what would be the produce of a single healthy fish in two
years, if, upon the protective principle, no egg became addled, and the germ of life were not thus prematurely cut
off, or where the fry were bred unhurt and unmolested ?
The natural hills where they breed are now more than half
of them destroyed, and the young become the prey of every
poacher, for such I deem the man who takes a young salmon fry.   The number produced would be enormous, and

would restore our fisheries to the enviable state they were in three centuries back, when, according to tradition, our rivers swarmed with good large salmon, and every kind of fish fit for the food of man. Without the artificial systematic arrangement I am urging upon the attention of my readers, our rivers must ultimately become depopulated; and let the proprietors of salmonries shut up their fisheries even for one, two, or more years, with the hope of their restoration, they will find themselves wofully mistaken in the end. The Rhine, which was never abused by over-fishing, formerly produced salmon of the largest and most luscious description : it lost its reputation for this breed of noble fish about the same time at which the Thames also became deserted ; yet salmon still pay an annual visit to the Rhine,—in proof whereof, witness the quantity of fine fish brought over to this country under the denomination of Dutch salmon, all taken as they are running into the mouth of the Rhine. A few salmon also arrive in the Thames, and may annually be observed making way and working up the quieter river Lea, which, instead of being pure water fitted to breed in, is no better than a sewer, and not a single egg of all their spawn is ever brought into life. Two years ago, it is true, a solitary grilse was killed at Teddington ; but how is it possible for any fish to pass such a formidable barrier as a six-feet-high puttock, even at high water, when it is known that the nimblest of salmon cannot reach that height in less than two leaps, at the least ?

These remarks will, I trust, lead my readers to consider this subject with attention : for, as I have said before, I look on the welfare of our fisheries as of national import-ance.   It may be a bold thing to say that the land is not more capable of producing food than the water ; but, how-ever heterodox an opinion it may seem to be, I cannot help holding it, and I am borne out, I believe, by natural-ists and religionists too : for, according to the Bible, the waters of this world were first populated by living crea-tures, and afterwards the lands.

It is a curious fact, also, that fish in spawning have their favourites ; but as the male favourite can only give his attentions during the process occasionally, the female is attended by many males, which is a wise provision of Nature for insuring a larger brood.   During the spawning season many contests take place among these competitors : the heavier fish has always the advantage, and only gives way to the smaller one when his milt is exhausted, although, at the spawning season, the whole water is charged with the fluids necessary for impregnation of the eggs of the breeding fish ; Nature has so beautifully arranged her work, that no two sorts of fish spawn at the same period, either in rivers, streams or ponds.   One species of fish indeed follows the other in rapid succession, showing that Nature is perfect in her plans, and disaffects the one power previous to the next coming forward, by which those anomalies in nature called hybrids are avoided in fresh water; and this fact will serve to show how easy a task it is to restore and regenerate fresh-water rivers and streams, to the advantage of the community at large.

Where a pond has the advantage of plentiful springs, so as to have an overflow, or has a small brook-stream passing through it, it has then everything needful for the assembling of trout, pike, perch, carp, tench, and other fish, in the same water, and all would thrive well together. I know of an instance of the kind near Guildford, in the county of Surrey, where the trout reached a large size, and all the other descriptions of fish were of fine quality. In fact, if a proper system were generally adopted by landed proprietors, an enormous amount of food might be supplied, which is now wanting, and a large revenue come into the pockets of the producers, which they now lose and neglect altogether; and all this might be done at very little cost. Remember for a moment that trout after their fourth year reach the weight of between three and four pounds; pike, perch, carp and tench rather heavier; and what may we not promise as the produce of water, when it forms part of the agrarian labours of a landed proprietor?

One great advantage in artificial spawning will be, that poaching will not be felt so severely as it is now: for the

yearly produce being kept up, and the streams still well
stocked with the produce of such fish as, in despite of the
destroyers, are fortunate enough to reach pure water for
spawning, we should, with very little watchfulness on our
parts, become so rich in fish, that the markets could be
supplied at a low figure, and at a large remunerating return
to the proprietors of the waters: so that quantity and
quality would thus go together; and I have no hesitation
in saying, that this system might be carried out with
equal surety of the same large annual return as I laid
down as the probable profits of a similar enterprize, in
my former Treatise upon fish-pends for carp, tench and
jack.

As far as salmon are concerned, the arrangement for artificial spawning, breeding and rearing, becomes of such
immense importance, that I consider it of national interest
and utility.   In the beginning of this treatise I have expressed my fears that all fresh-water fish would gradually
become extinct, from the several well-founded causes
named; and these are since confirmed by parties who have
borne their testimony to the destruction daily going on in a
stream where the sewerage of villages is not the principal
source of the evil; and still the eggs are suffocated during
the process of incubation.   What must not the spawn of
every description of fish suffer when it is deposited in the
turgid waters passing through large metropolitan towns

and thickly-inhabited counties, where access is cut off to the pure springs of water !

As regards salmon, if I am rightly informed by a gentleman at Gloucester, who is a proprietor of twelve miles of the river Severn, the grilse spawns in September and October ; the salmon in October, November and December. The young fish issue from the egg in from 100 to 120 days, according as the warmth of the water may have varied, which at that time of the year, from cold, rain or snow, it frequently does; the process of incubation being retarded in proportion to the effects produced by the nitrous quality of snow-water, which reduces the temperature from 55° to 30°, and that in a few hours ; and when a large mass of snow falls into a spring-stream, it acts like salt combined with snow, and freezes all before it. Oyster-beds for miles are sometimes from this cause totally destroyed in one night; for when this occurs all fish retire to the deeps. Some streams, from this, in conjunction with other causes, freeze upwards from their very beds in the shallows, and it is there where most fish prefer to spawn : so that every egg is directly destroyed; but, fortunately, this extreme case is not of frequent occurrence, although I have observed it in more instances than one. The ice forms on the bed of the stream, and rises upwards to the surface as the water recovers its original temperature. There are parts of the Colne where this can be observed. As grilse spawn so much earlier than salmon, being maiden fish, it follows that the produce of their spawn is much earlier ready for migration, and begin to run in April, when they are about fifteen months old.   I have omitted to mention, in its proper place, the interesting fact, that the shell of the young fry of salmon adheres to the umbilical cord for nearly a calendar month, which brings the fish to 130 days from the deposit of the egg before he can hunt for his food, and the smolt is beyond a yearling before he is strong enough to take to the salt water; and when this change, is made he bids adieu to fresh-water feeding for ever.   A salmon or a grilse, returning to its native river to spawn, feeds no more on what was formerly its food, though it sports with flies, and will now and then take a minnow or a lobworm.   No sort of food is ever found in the maw of the salmon when cap-tured in fresh water; but when taken at the mouths of rivers, or on the coast making towards them, the remains of small fry are frequently found among the contents of the stomach.   The salmon and grilse, too, when taken at the mouth of a river, are of different flesh and flavour to those taken up-stream, the former being firm, brittle of flesh, and of large flake; but when taken in the latter, the flesh is weedy, thin of flake, and wanting in fat, and is of course greatly affected by the enlarged size of the roe or milt. Mr. Young, of Sutherlandshire, writing on this subject lately in a weekly publication, says, that "each salmon, upon his second return to his native stream, will weigh from nine to sixteen pounds weight, at which period," he says, " the fish can be only two years old." What may we not hope from this circumstance, if we resort to the artificial protective principle I am advocating ?

Regarding the period called fence-months, I must strongly recommend that, in all salmonries, the strictest protection shall be given to the brood at the time when they are going down-stream for the sea; for it is at that critical period that the skilful fly-fisher can, with very little trouble, fill his creel with the smolts or young salmon, who would, if not thus untimely taken, become grilse in about four months more. The destruction done by these fishermen may be computed when I mention that, if they make use of many flies at the same time, smolts will be taken by every hook. Again, on the return of the fish from sea, the shameful practice of placing pots, as they are termed, in the narrow passes at the mouths of rivers, ought to be done away with : in the first place, because they retard the progress of the fish ; and, in the second place, they afford a favourable opportunity to the porpoise, which feeds largely upon salmon. If this system of pots were set aside, the porpoise would not be able to follow them up and take them so easily in the brack water. A curious instance of the perseverance of a porpoise, when chasing his prey, occurred a few years since off the Isle of Dogs, in the Thames.

He was close up in the wake of a good-sized salmon, when
the latter made two or three extraordinary leaps, and in
the last threw himself on the mud, and was picked up by a
waterman, who rejoiced greatly at his prize, while the porpoise, running as close as he could safely to the shore, was
disappointed of his game.   A salmon, chased by a small
porpoise in the Severn, leaped over a pot and escaped,
while the porpoise blundered into it and broke it to pieces.
I have seen salmon much lacerated by the sharp teeth of
the porpoise ; and it is a curious fact, that when a salmon,
or indeed any other sort of fish, is thus lacerated, it immediately becomes sickly, and more especially the salmon,
which is a fish of an irritable, nervous habit, and in a very
few days loses flesh and flavour.   All working fishermen
are aware of this circumstance, and get rid of any wounded
fish they may net, even in preference to those they may
have already had in their salmon boxes.

Another severe hindrance to salmon, in making up for
the heads of rivers to reach the waters fit for spawning in,
are the weirs, some of which are too formidable for the fish
to overcome, unless a strong flood or fresh comes down to
their assistance.   If the weirs in most rivers were either
much altered, or, better still, abolished altogether, in that
case—what with natural spawning and artificial spawning,
protection of the smolt going down to sea, and the unin-
terrupted return afterwards of grilse and salmon to their

birth-places—the produce would be enormous: for, as I have said before, the salmon is not like any other fresh-water fish, and takes little or none of the fresh-water food after it has been once to sea; and therefore does not live at the cost of the other species of fish in the same river. Though I am as fond of handling my fly-rod as any man, I strongly recommend that no angler shall be allowed to fish in any salmon river, to the destruction of the fry, or kill any migratory species that have not been once to salt water; and further, that all fisheries be vigilantly watched, to put down all unlawful nets and unlawful arts: assured as I am that the proprietors of fisheries would soon find out the advantages of all this care. The trout grows fast, and is good food; but in the Thames it is frequently taken at a time of the year when it is out of season, and easily captured, from the voracity of its appetite when recovering from spawning. Thames anglers, impatient for their sport, begin to fish by spinning a minnow or bleak in the month of March; and should they take a ten-pounder, which is not uncommon, boast of having captured a fine fish, whereas in fact it is only fit to be thrown away, being full of worms and flabby of flesh. Were such a fish left for three months longer, it would not only have increased in weight, but it would have been worth some-thing, as it would have been in season. The spawn of such a fish would be about 6000 or 7000 eggs. In taking a trout at that time there is neither art nor science, the fish being still so weak from spawning—for large fish spawn very late—that it has not the power to contend against the rod and line, which it would have had in June.

Here again, in this improper taking of trout out of season, the want of a proper system of protection is forcibly felt; and this same shield of protection is wanting as well for all other fresh-water fish : for were the artificial principle and protective arrangement extended to them, their increase would be enormous. In the stream which I have laid down and attended to, for example, even roach grow to the great weight of from one and a half to two pounds in their fourth season; and this weight is, I believe, unprecedented elsewhere. This shows at once what protection and management will do for fisheries; and that fisheries, like farms, when looked to systematically, will flourish, and, when neglected, fail.

Having, I hope, however hastily and cursorily, shown some of the private advantages of artificial spawning and protection of every species of fish, I will next draw the attention of my readers to the public advantages which would accrue if the same attention were paid to all the rivers in the United Kingdom; for if my data be looked into, and if they are they will bear investigation, and my system carried out by owners of fisheries, we might well calculate upon a greatly-augmented increase of employment, a new source of revenue, and a large supply of wholesome food, at a price so reasonable as to bring it within the means of the poorest classes.

The stream which I have made my model is dragged two or three times in the season, to get rid of the coarse fish and give room to the rising brood; and all streams will be the better for this annual removal of the large fish, a rule applicable to all waters, which would soon tell in the pockets of their proprietors. There is nothing worse than a piece of water overstocked.

The conflicting interests in salmonries give rise to much jealousy, and to much undoing by one proprietor of any good which may be attempted by another: so much so, that I despair of seeing anything effectually done for the benefit of all by the exertions of individual proprietors; but if the system of artificial spawning which I am recommending conld, by any means, be carried out by a company of these proprietors, holding shares in proportion to the extent of their waters, the obstacles which now stand sturdily in the way of improvement would be removed at once and for ever, and the company would be well repaid for the outlaying of their capital.

As I have said, in an earlier page of this little work, it is neither the passage of ships and steam-vessels, nor the gas-works, which have injuriously affected the breeding of fish; for the vessels of burthen are moored in the brack

and mixed water, and the steamers simply wash the mud
farther down stream, out of the way of the clear water in
which trout and salmon breed : steam navigation so far,
therefore, is rather an advantage than a hindrance to the
work.   And as to the gas-works, every particle of residue
derived from the distillation of coal is a source of profit :
the ammoniacal liquor is sold to make carbonate and mu-
riate of ammonia, the sulphate of lime for manure, the tar
for various useful outdoor purposes ; and consequently
very little refuse passes to the rivers or streams.   Again, I
will make a comparison of the Thames with the Tyne : no
salmon are now caught in the Thames, but though the
Tyne has many alkali works on its shores from Newcastle
downwards,—and alkali is death to every species of fish,—
yet it abounds with salmon.   How is it that, with these
destructive manufactories on its banks, and in despite of
the swarms of steam-boats and tugs ever passing up and
down that river, it is still a good fishery ?   Why, simply
because salmon and all other fish migrating from water to
water never stop on their way, but push forward, and that
at a fast rate, till their intended journey, for which Nature
has prepared them, is completed : for, as I have said, salmon being very swift, soon pass through the water which
is offensive, and then run for the pure springs fit for
spawning.

As birds of migratory habits, previous to the time of

travel, get extremely fat, and can bear the want of food for
many days till their flight is accomplished, so is it with
fish which migrate ; and this fact will account for salmon
being finer in flesh when taken off the mouth of a river,
and better flavoured in brackish than in fresh water.
Again, Thames salmon have a very short distance to travel
to get out of bad water into good, and leave the shipping
and bugbear steam-boats behind them.   We will take
Woolwich Reach, always brackish water, and get up to
Hammersmith, a distance of twenty miles, which salmon
in good health and full vigour would traverse in less than
three-quarters of an hour.

1 will now recall the attention of my readers to the plan
which I propose for increasing the food of man, by restoring the stock in rivers. To second the artificial spawning
principle, I propose that no pots or traps shall be permit-
ted in the salt or brack water, so that salmon in their mi-
grations may descend their native streams unmolested;
and that where weirs are positively required, they should
be made upon the principle previously described, so as to
be easily surmounted.

Artificial spawning for salmon is extremely simple : all
that is required is, to obtain as many female fish, or spawn-
ers, as are deemed sufficient to produce spawn enough to
restock the river.   One male, or milter, is able to impart
the germinating principle to the eggs of a dozen full-grown

females. The principal point to be attended to is, to take
the female at the right time, and this is when she is working high up stream; for though some females return nearly
ready to spawn, the greater number make for the springs
some time before they are full-gone and ripe for parturition.   You may easily know when a fish is full up and in
condition to have her eggs taken from her, by looking out
for the redness and protrusion of the vent; and this must
be particularly attended to, or the mother may be destroyed
in the operation.

To spawn artificially, first, a clear, clean, unadulterated
spring must be found, at a temperature of 54° to 56°, which
can be so hemmed back as to form a good fall of water:
then the boxes, of any size, according to the amount of
fish required, must be placed one by another, and so arranged that the water shall pass from one to the other;
for, as each box receives its spawn in succession regularly, it is essentially necessary that the flow of water
shall be at the command of the operator. The boxes must
be made water-tight, with lids to all; and the first box
should be placed one or two inches higher than the second,
so that the flow shall fall into each box in regular succession, and form an artificial ripple, by which the egg is
affected on the artificial hill in exactly the same way as on
its natural one. On sunny days it is advisable to open the
lids, and let the rays of light pass to them; for though the

egg is buried in the shingle, it is not at such a depth but that light affects it, and that sensibly. The use of lids to the spawn-boxes is to prevent water-fowl and herons from peculation, and keep the prying curiosity of individuals from disturbing the eggs, which is pretty sure to end in their becoming addled. The boxes being water-tight, the size I recommend should be about four feet long to from twelve to eighteen inches broad and nine inches deep. You then charge them with shingle, or very coarse, well-washed gravel, divested of all sand, to about six inches deep, which will leave a flow of water over the shingle of about two inches. The end of each box falling into the succeeding one must have an aperture left for the water, which, with the help of a small flange, is shot into the next, on the principle of a weir, so that the end of each box would be but eight inches deep; and by these means box after box will be filled with succession spawn, according to the take of the fish as they ascend for spawning.

The small fish are the first to spawn, the larger ascend later; but it is always advisable to obtain, if possible, a young male and an old female, as the brood are always the finest—to which subject I shall soon allude more at length. The last box of all in these artificial spawning-beds, or hills, must differ from the spawning-boxes in being three times as broad, to form an eddy, and deeper by three or four inches; and in this, which is the receiving-box for the

brood, less shingle or gravel should be placed, that there
may be the more room for water.　At the end of this box
a perforated zinc plate is to be placed, of the width and
immediately opposite to the flow from the preceding spawn-
box next to it : so that the water, being prevented from
passing off too freely, forms an eddy in the back part of the
same ; and it is into this box that the brood will descend
as soon as the egg-shell has dropped from their bodies.
Here all the young fry are easily and safely captured, where,
if any other system were adopted, thousands would be
destroyed, from the extremely fragile and tender nature of
their frames, to which a bruise, however slight, is fatal ; and
therefore, in removing them from the artificial bed to the
nursery-stream, great care must be taken, or thousands will
be destroyed.　Here, in this nursery, they remain undis-
turbed for the time necessary to bring them up, which is
from fifteen to eighteen months, and then they may be
turned into the river.　If the brood is salmon, they depart
of themselves, if the barrier to the nursery be removed ;
if trout, or some other brood, it is best to take them and
transfer them to different parts of the fishery.　By this
fostering system, we know to a certainty what stock we
have in hand ; and were this plan diligently and annually
followed out, we could reclaim all the rivers and streams
in the United Kingdom.

Six years have I successfully carried out this arrange-

ment with trout in a fishery not far from London, which is
now the richest stream in the South of England.   The
principle of artificial spawning I have been acquainted
with as far back as 1815 ; and I rely so confidently on the
results which would ensue were it carried out, that I give
my experience ·as data to go upon, and now proceed with
the practical part of the subject.   Premising the spring of
water is found, the boxes in order, and the yearling brook
arranged,—and this must be particularly attended to, as it
affords the main or chief protection to the brood,—then,
in the early part of October, you begin to drag for the
grilse, which are ready to spawn.   Presuming, therefore,
that you have taken a spawner or milter in or near the
proper state, to be certain of this the vent must be ex-
amined, and upon its appearing of a pear-shaped form,
protruding and red, it may be considered in a proper condition for expressing the eggs and milt.   If they are not
in this state, or fairly up, on no account undertake the operation, as in so doing some of the soft internal parts may
be ruptured and the fish destroyed, whilst the eggs untimely taken would be useless.   In case the fish are not
forward enough, they should be kept in tanks in the river
for a few days, for at this time they do not feed.   Should
the fish be all right, take a large earthenware pan, with
about two quarts of the spring water at bottom, and, holding the female fish up by the gill-covers, draw your hand

D

downwards from the pectoral fins to the anal point. This
must not be done roughly, but with sufficient force to ex-
pel the eggs from the ovarium into the pan. The same
process is then to be applied to the milter immediately afterwards, rather nearer the vent, the whole milt not being
ready at one time ; but it is not necessary to obtain a large
quantity of the vivifying fluid from him, as a very little of
it diluted with water is enough for thousands of eggs. I
have known the spawner, when perfectly to her time, shoot
all her eggs upon merely holding her up ; but this I attri-
buted to fear. On blending the milt with the spawn, a very
interesting change takes place in the egg. Before the fluid
of the milter is added, all the eggs are of a very brilliant
reddish yellow ; the instant it is blended, the outer cuticle
of the egg becomes opaque and lustreless. As soon as the
milt is expressed in the water with the eggs, the whole
must be agitated with the hand for about a minute, and
then the operation is completed. You may now place the
eggs upon the shingle, taking great care, however, that
they do not lay one upon another, and cover them up
with fresh shingle, two inches deep, letting the spring water
flow freely over them ; and in a hundred days you have
the fry.

As this is a project for producing food, and not merely
for furnishing amusement, though they may be combined,
I must urge strongly on the breeder the positive necessity

of keeping the spawning-boxes particularly clean. Should
any film, from the nature of the spring water, form therein,
it is advisable to take a hair-broom and sweep carefully
and lightly over the shingle daily ; and, should there be
anything likely to impede incubation, the flow of water will
carry it away.

Upon this system, trout require only fifty days for incubation ; jack, perch, roach and dace, forty-two days ; carp
and tench the same time ; and as the spawn of the two
last-named fish is deposited near the surface of the water,
they are bred in ponds, but they may be removed to
streams, where they thrive.   In trout-streams, where the
water is almost all spring, it is absolutely necessary that
some provision should be made for feeding this fish, especially where there are no larvæ or insects ; and this can
only be done by breeding coarse fish in the streams, or in
ponds or stews, so formed that they can be emptied into the
stream, or the stream be let in, and wash them out, at in-
tervals.   In the North of Scotland, I understand that the
trout of some lakes and streams are in season not more
than two months out of the twelve, and that this is owing
entirely to their want of proper food ; and where this is
the case the larger fish prey upon the spawn-beds, or chase
the smaller, so that over-exertion keeps them lean and out of
condition.   Reverse this order of things by artificial feeding, and what is the result ?—an enormous increase of pro-

duce for the food of the country, and a splendid stock for
future operations in breeding and rearing.

After the successful experiments I have myself made, I
have no hesitation in saying, that if thinking minds will
aid and assist in working out this great practical problem,
we may produce and supply an enormous amount of food
to our poorer fellow-creatures, at a cheap rate to them, and
at very little trouble and cost to ourselves.   It is no chi-
merical good I am advocating : I am plainly, and in true
terms, relating a tale of experience, and should be sorry to
advance a single assertion which could not be sustained by
irrefragable evidence.   All the fresh waters of these United
Kingdoms, it is not too much to say, are grossly neglected,
and the rivers especially are imperfectly understood ; but
I hope to hear shortly that the broad hints I have given
for obviating these evils have aroused the energies of men
who are well-wishers to their country, so that they will
undertake a work which will be profitable to themselves,
and that they will attend more closely to the fisheries in
fresh water.   In our fisheries, salmon is first in rank ; trout
the second ; grayling follows ; and then the coarse fish,
pike, perch, carp, tench, roach and dace, come as a matter
of course : these are not to be despised, though light in
food in comparison with the first.

It will be seen that, by this system of artificial spawning,
breeding and rearing of fish, depleted rivers running into

the sea can be recovered in the short time of two years, and turned to large account. Smaller streams, on the same principles, may be restored with equal certainty, but after a longer term of labour and attention : for four years must elapse before the first brood will be fit to be taken, which time expiring, every fish of that age in the stream will be in good order for the market; but previous to this time they furnish good sport to the angler. At that age the fish, being then about three pounds weight, should be taken out and sent to market, when he is in high perfection, leaving the then forward-coming brood as successors in their place. In fresh-water streams, where the fish do not migrate, no fish should be allowed to attain a greater weight than from three to four pounds, for this reason—as they get larger they consume much more food in proportion to their smaller companions, and keep down the stock by destroying the egg or spawn, as well as the young fry. There is no exception in fish preying upon spawn, if they can get at it ; one sort is not one jot less voracious than another— leather-mouthed or sharp-toothed, they are all alike, and are not at all particular whether it is their own production or that of other species: the older a fish gets the more destructive he becomes ; and therefore these should be the first to be removed from a fishery, excepting always a few for brood.

When fisheries are well up, it is advisable to take all the

large common fish out by judicious netting, as the food they uselessly consume will then go to support fish of better qualities.   I do not allude either to grilse or salmon, but decidedly to the smolt, trout, and other good freshwater fish.   Trout require abundance of food all the year round ; and this should be furnished by coarse fish, the young of which are the food they like best and thrive upon.

I have now to hope, in conclusion, that the readers of this treatise will give its arguments and statements their best attention ; and if I have not gone deep enough into the merits of fisheries, I trust that men with more power of research will follow up the subject, pursue it through all its issues, and prosper : for in this age of knowledge it is greatly to be regretted that water should not be cultivated as much as land, and more especially when it is matter of fact that water is far more capable of producing abundance of food than any other element in the great laboratory of Nature.   Why, then, should such a source of plenty be neglected ?

THE END.

BOOKS PUBLISHED BY MR. VAN VOORST.

The Illustrations to the Works enumerated in the following List have been designed or drawn and engraved expressly for the Works they respectively embellish, and they are never used for other Works.

HERALDRY OF FISH. By THOMAS MOULE. The Engravings, 205 in number, are from Stained Glass, Tombs, Sculpture and Carving, Medals and Coins, Rolls of Arms and Pedigrees. 8vo., price 21s. A few on large paper (royal 8vo.) for colouring, price 2l. 2s.

GEOLOGY : Introductory, Descriptive, and Practical. By DAVID THOMAS ANSTED, M.A., F.R.S.; Fellow of Jesus College, Cambridge; Professor of Geology in King's College, London. 2 Vols. 8vo., with numerous Illustrative Engravings, price 2l. 2s.

THE BIRDS OF JAMAICA. By P. H. GOSSE, Author of the "Canadian Naturalist," &c. Post 8vo, price 10s.

   ILLUSTRATIONS to the new Species described in this Work, in about 15 Parts, at 2s. 6d. Each Part will contain Four Birds Coloured.

OBSERVATIONS IN NATURAL HISTORY ; with a Calendar of Periodic Phenomena. By the REV. LEONARD JENYNS, M.A., F.L.S. Post 8vo., 10s. 6d.

ILLUSTRATIONS OF INSTINCT, Deduced from the Habits of British Animals. By JONATHAN COUCH, F.L.S., Member of the Royal Geological Society and of the Royal Institution of Cornwall, &c. Post 8vo., 8s. 6d.

THE ANCIENT WORLD ; or, Picturesque Sketches of Creation. By D. T. ANSTED, M.A., F R.S., F.G.S., Professor of Geology in King's College, London, &c., &c. A New Edition, Post 8vo., with 149 Illustrations, 10s. 6d.

OUTLINES OF STRUCTURAL AND PHYSIOLOGICAL BOTANY. By ARTHUR HENFREY, F.L.S., Lecturer on Botany at the Middlesex Hospital; late Botanist to the Geological Survey of the United Kingdom. With 18 Plates, Foolscap 8vo., 10s. 6d.

A MANUAL OF BRITISH BOTANY; containing the Flowering Plants and Ferns, arranged according to the Natural Orders. By CHARLES C. BABINGTON, M.A., F.L.S., F.Z.S., &c. Second Edition, 12mo., 10s.

FIRST STEPS TO ANATOMY. By JAMES L. DRUMMOND, M.D., Professor of Anatomy and Physiology in the Belfast Royal Institution. With 12 Illustrative Plates, 12 mo., 5s.

THE NATURAL HISTORY OF STAFFORDSHIRE, comprising its Geology, Zoology, Botany, and Meteorology ; also its Antiquities Topography, Manufactures, &c. By ROBERT GARNER, F.L.S. Illustrated, 8vo., 1l. 1s.

THE HONEY BEE ; its Natural History, Physiology, and Management. By EDWARD BEVAN, M.D. A new Edition, 12mo., with Illustrations, 10s. 6d.

ON THE GROWTH OF PLANTS IN CLOSELY-GLAZED CASES. By N. B. WARD, F.L.S. 8vo., 5s.

A FAMILIAR INTRODUCTION TO THE HISTORY OF INSECTS. By EDWARD NEWMAN, F.L.S., F.Z.S., &c. 8vo., with nearly 100 Illustrations, price 12s.

WHITE'S NATURAL HISTORY OF SELBORNE. A new Edition, with Notes by the REV. LEONARD JENYNS, M.A., F.L.S. Foolscap 8vo., Illustrated, 7s. 6d.

THE ISLE OF MAN ; its History, Physical, Ecclesiastical, Civil, and Legendary. By the REV. J. G. CUMMING, M.A., F.G.S., Vice-Principal of King William's College, Castletown. Post 8vo., with Illustrations, 12s. 6d.

PROFESSOR OWEN ON THE ARCHETYPE AND HOMOLOGIES OF THE VERTEBRATE SKELETON. 8vo., 10s.

A SYSTEMATIC CATALOGUE OF THE EGGS OF BRITISH BIRDS, arranged with a View to supersede the use of Labels for 'Eggs. By the Rev. S. C. Malan, M.A., M.A.S. On writing-paper. 8vo., 8s. 6d.

RARE AND REMARKABLE ANIMALS OF SCOTLAND, Represented from Living Subjects : with Practical Observations on their Nature. By Sir John Graham Dalyell, Bart. Vol. First, 53 Coloured Plates, 4to., 3l. 3s.

THE FARMER'S BOY AND OTHER RURAL TALES AND POEMS. By Robert Bloomfield. With 13 Illustrations by Sidney Cooper, R.A., Horsley, Frederick Tayler, and Thomas Webster, R.A. Foolscap 8vo., 7s. 6d.

A FAMILIAR INTRODUCTION TO THE STUDY OF POLARIZED LIGHT ; with a Description of, and Instructions for Using, the Table and Hydro-Oxygen Polariscope and Microscope. By Charles Woodward, F.R.S. 8vo., Illustrated, 3s.

THE NATURAL HISTORY OF GREAT BRITAIN. This Series of Works is Illustrated by many Hundred Engravings ; every Species has been Drawn and Engraved under the immediate inspection of the Authors ; the best Artists have been employed, and no care or expense has been spared. A few copies on larger paper, royal 8vo.

THE QUADRUPEDS, by Professor Bell. 1l. 8s.

THE BIRDS, by Mr. Yarrell. Second Edition, 3 vols., 4l. 14s. 6d.

COLOURED ILLUSTRATIONS OF THE EGGS OF BIRDS, by Mr. Hewitson. 2 vols., 4l. 10s.

THE REPTILES, by Professor Bell. Second Edition, shortly.

THE FISHES, by Mr. Yarrell. Second Edition, 2 vols., 3l.

THE CRUSTACEA, by Professor Bell. Now in Course of Publication, in Parts at 2s. 6d.

THE STARFISHES, by Professor Edward Forbes. 15s.

THE ZOOPHYTES, by Dr. Johnston. Second Ed., 2 vols., 2l. 2s.

THE MOLLUSCOUS ANIMALS AND THEIR SHELLS, by Professor Ed. Forbes and Mr. Hanley. Now in Course of Publication, in Parts at 2s. 6d.; or Large Paper, with the Plates Coloured, 5s.

THE FOREST TREES, by Mr. Selby. 28s.

THE FERNS AND ALLIED PLANTS, by Mr. Newman. 25s.

THE FOSSIL MAMMALS AND BIRDS, by Professor Owen. 1l. 11s. 6d.

A GENERAL OUTLINE OF THE ANIMAL KINGDOM, by Professor T. Rymer Jones. 8vo., 1l. 18s.

JOHN VAN VOORST, PATERNOSTER ROW.

BOOKS ON FISHES, FISHING, &c.

A TREATISE ON THE MANAGEMENT OF FRESH WATER FISH, with a View to making them a Source of Profit to Landed Proprietors. By GOTTLIEB BOCCIUS. In 8vo. price 5s. with a Woodcut of the Spiegel, or Mirror Carp.

HERALDRY OF FISH. By THOMAS MOULE. Nearly 600 Families are noticed in this Work, and besides the several descriptions of Fish, Fishing-nets, and Boats, are included also Mermaids, Tritons, and Shell-fish. Nearly seventy Ancient Seals are described, and upwards of twenty Subjects in stained Glass. The Engravings, 205 in Number, are from stained Glass, Tombs, Sculpture, and Carving, Medals, and Coins, Rolls of Arms, and Pedigrees. 8vo. price 21s., a few on large paper (royal 8vo.), for colouring, price 2l. 2s.

AN ANGLER'S RAMBLES. By EDWARD JESSE, Esq., F.L.S. Author of "Gleanings in Natural History." Contents.—Thames Fishing—Trolling in Staffordshire—Perch Fishing Club—Two Days' Fly-fishing on the Test—Luckford Fishing Club—Grayling Fishing—A Visit to Oxford—The Country Clergyman. In post 8vo. price 10s. 6d. cloth.

" Our readers are well acquainted with Mr. Jesse, and the present work is in his own peculiar and pleasant style; there is the same love of nature, the same good feeling, and the same variety of anecdote, told in his own lively manner."—*Literary Gazette.*

A HISTORY OF BRITISH FISHES. By WILLIAM YARRELL, Esq., F.L.S., V.P.Z.S. This Work, which contains a complete History of the Ichthyology of Great Britain, including many Species never before noticed, is embellished with FIGURES of FISHES, mostly taken from the Objects themselves, and ILLUSTRATIVE VIGNETTES, drawn and engraved by the most eminent Artists. Second Edition. In 2 vols. 8vo. price 3l. Illustrated by nearly 500 beautiful Woodcuts.

" This book ought to be largely circulated, not only on account of its scientific merits—though these, as we have in part shewn, are great and signal—but because it is popularly written throughout, and therefore likely to excite general attention to a subject which ought to be held as one of primary importance. Every one is interested about fishes—the political economist, the epicure, the merchant, the man of science, the angler, the poor, the rich. We hail the appearance of this book as the dawn of a new era in the Natural History of England."—*Quarterly Review*, No. 116.

Also by Mr. YARRELL.

A PAPER ON THE GROWTH OF THE SALMON IN FRESH WATER. With six Illustrations of the Fish of the natural Size, exhibiting its Structure and exact Appearance at various Stages during the first two Years. 12s. sewed.

NOTES ON NETS; or, The Quincunx practically considered. To which are added, Miscellaneous Memoranda. By the Hon. and Rev. CHARLES BATHURST, LL.D., late Fellow of All Souls' College, Oxford. With Engravings, price 4s. in boards.

" Every branch of art or manufacture has had its guide, or its catechism, or its alphabet, and so on; but the art of netting seems, by some accident, to have entirely escaped the notice of the press; although, in truth, it is the art which furnishes us with much wholesome food through its immediate instrumentality, urges men to industry, and can be practised without any very great outlay of capital to the maker."—*Extract from Preface.*

JOHN VAN VOORST, 1, PATERNOSTER ROW.

CPSIA information can be obtained
at www.ICGtesting.com
Printed in the USA
BVHW071623280119
538839BV00028B/2304/P